HOME SWEET HOME

a picture book by Maureen Roffey

Coward-McCann, Inc.

New York

Does a cat live in a kennel?

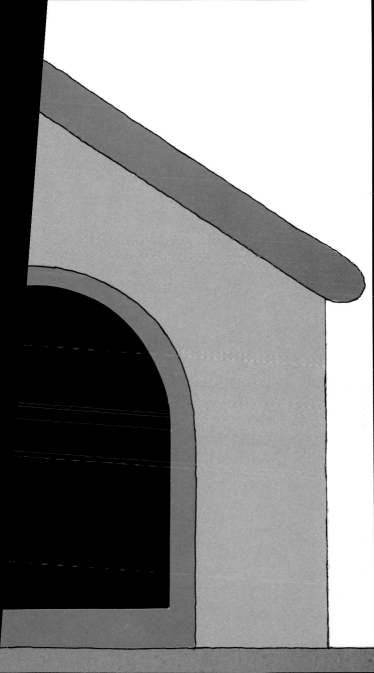

No! A dog lives in a kennel,

of course.

Do butterflies live in a hive?

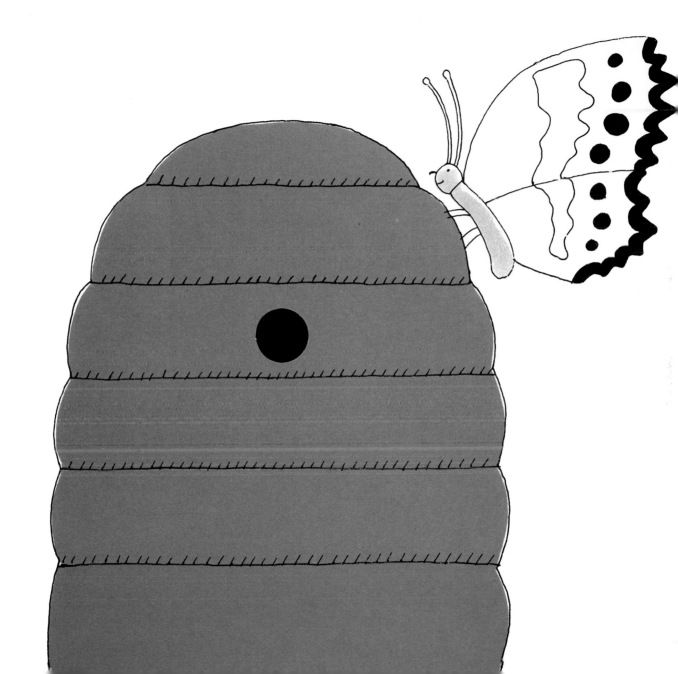

No! Bees live in a hive.

Does Alice live in this coop?

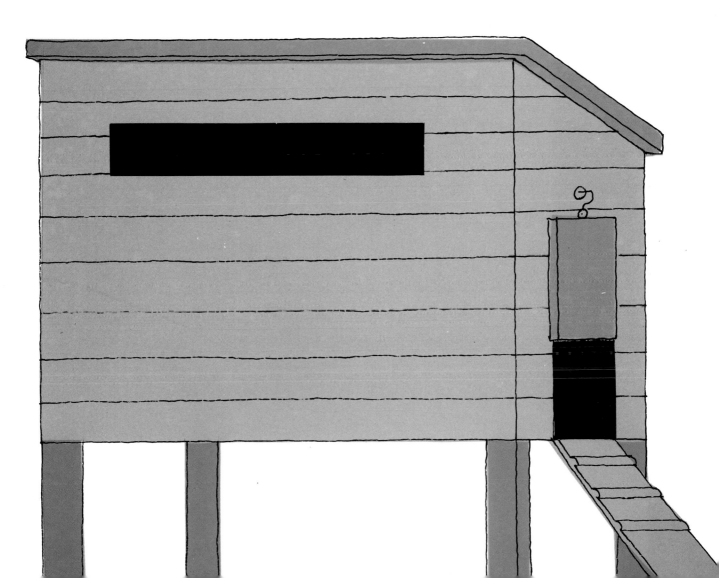

No! Her hens do

Does a cow live in a stable?

Do rabbits live down a hole?

Yes! And it's called a warren.

And who
lives here?